THE ROMAN EMPIRE
The World's First Superpower

Dedication

Once again to Hilary Alexander, care-worker in Gloucester Park Day Centre, Larne.

THE ROMAN EMPIRE
The World's First Superpower

Michael Sheane

ARTHUR H. STOCKWELL LTD
Torrs Park, Ilfracombe, Devon, EX34 8BA
Established 1898
www.ahstockwell.co.uk

© Michael Sheane, 2021
First published in Great Britain, 2021

The moral rights of the author have been asserted.

All rights reserved.
No part of this publication may be reproduced
or transmitted in any form or by any means,
electronic or mechanical, including photocopy,
recording, or any information storage and
retrieval system, without permission
in writing from the copyright holder.

British Library Cataloguing-in-Publication Data.
A catalogue record for this book is available
from the British Library.

Arthur H. Stockwell Ltd bears no responsibility
for the accuracy of information recorded in this book.

ISBN 978-0-7223-5104-8
Printed in Great Britain by
Arthur H. Stockwell Ltd
Torrs Park   Ilfracombe
Devon EX34 8BA

By the same author:
Ulster & Its Future After the Troubles (1977)
Ulster & The German Solution (1978)
Ulster & The British Connection (1979)
Ulster & The Lords of the North (1980)
Ulster & The Middle Ages (1982)
Ulster & St Patrick (1984)
The Twilight Pagans (1990)
Enemy of England (1991)
The Great Siege (2002)
Ulster in the Age of Saint Comgall of Bangor (2004)
Ulster Blood (2005)
King William's Victory (2006)
Ulster Stock (2007)
Famine in the Land of Ulster (2008)
Pre-Christian Ulster (2009)
The Glens of Antrim (2010)
Ulster Women – A Short History (2010)
The Invasion of Ulster (2010)
Ulster in the Viking Age (2011)
Ulster in the Eighteenth Century (2011)
Ulster in the History of Ireland (2012)
Rathlin Island (2013)
Saint Patrick's Missionary Journeys in Ireland (2015)
The Story of Carrickfergus (2015)
Ireland's Holy Places (2016)
The Conqueror of the North (2017)
The Story of Holywell Hospital: A Country Asylum (2018)
Patrick: A Saint for All Seasons (2019)
The Picts: The Painted People (2019)
Pictland: The Conversion to Christianity of a Pagan Race (2020)
Irish & Scottish Dalriada (2020)

The Roman Empire

The World's First Superpower

Rome was founded in 753 BC as the central city of the Latin people. To the north lay the lands of the Indo-European Etruscans and to the south the Greek colonies and other Italian tribes. Rome became a republic in 510 BC. By 266 BC Rome controlled the Italian peninsula and then moved into Sicily to oppose Carthaginian power. Victory in the Punic Wars (264–146 BC) gave Rome an empire that included Spain, Sardinia, Corsica, Sicily and Tunisia, with annexations in northern Italy and areas of southern France.

Military leaders such as Julius Caesar acquired Gaul, Greece and other tribal territories as far away as Egypt and Palestine. His heir, Augustus, in 27 BC extended the Roman Empire over the Alps and to the rivers Rhine and Danube. The empire reached its final extent under Marcus Aurelius with the Pax Romana. Under the Emperor Diocletian the empire reached its widest extent in AD 285–305, but it ultimately fell to barbarian tribes like the Huns, who sacked Rome in 410.

The Etruscans were an early people that inhabited ancient Italy, having their own language and civilization.

Rome was situated in Etruscan territory, and the Etruscans may have dominated Rome until the kings of the city, some say in 396 BC. Etruscan influence gradually declined as Roman power increased.

Celtic origins date back to the fifth and eighth centuries BC, with movements into modern France, Britain and Iberia. By the fourth century BC the Celts were making movements into northern Italy and eventually into Turkey. The Celts had a distinctive art form, producing beautiful metalwork; and of course they were also great warriors.

There were a number of languages in Italy, but local tongues died out and Latin took precedence over Greek in Roman colonies in southern Italy. The Venetians had their own language along with other non-Latin regions.

Now this was the age of the rise of Rome, but Rome remained under Etruscan influence for almost 250 years from 753 BC; it controlled strategic positions on the River Tiber. For 200 years Rome gradually extended its influence, and the last Etruscans were overthrown in 510 BC, when Rome became a republic. At the Battle of Aricia, in 506 BC, Rome achieved independence. By 266 BC Rome controlled the territories north of the River Rubicon, conferring its citizenship throughout this region.

Now followed the Punic Wars (264–146 BC), involving Carthage, a powerful city state. It was inevitable that these great powers would conflict with each other. The result was that Rome obtained a number of victories, leading to the acquisition of Sicily, Sardinia and Corsica and Rome's undisputed control of the Mediterranean. The Carthaginians under Hannibal marched with a great army across the Alps to attack Rome from northern

Italy, and they almost defeated the Romans under their general, Scipio. The Battle of Zama was decisive in the Punic Wars, taking place on 19 October 202 BC. The Carthaginians sued for peace and the terms of the treaty were so severe that Carthage was never again able to challenge the might of Rome. The eastern Mediterranean in 100 BC saw the Roman Empire expanding in the east, coming into contact with empires like that of the Seleucids; Egypt was still an independent power, but the entire region was ready for a Roman takeover. In 55 BC the Roman Empire was still expanding; most of Europe was coming under the power of Rome. This was the age of the First Triumvirate, formed in 60 BC, consisting of Caesar, Pompey and Crassus, each of them controlling his own territory; they completely dominated Roman politics.

Under the emperors the city of Rome was the largest urban centre of its time, roughly the size of London in the nineteenth century, with a population of about one million. The constant noise of horses and other traffic led to proposals to ban traffic at night – horses and carts. Rome is situated on seven hills and had vast buildings – the Colosseum, the Forum and the Pantheon. It had all the facilities of a civilized city, including theatres, libraries, shops, marketplaces and functional sewers. The rich lived in elegant residences, but the lower and middle classes had to live in apartments in the city centre.

On the war front there were Caesar's campaigns in Gaul from 53 to 48 BC. He had undertaken these campaigns to boost his political career and to pay off his massive debts, but one must not underestimate the importance of Gaul to the Roman Empire.

Caesar also sent two expeditions to Britain. On the first attempt he stayed for only about a year; he returned the following year, when he defeated the powerful British kings. This kept him in the public eye.

A great battle took place in Greece between rivals to power in Rome. Known as the Battle of Pharsalia, it was fought in 48 BC between Caesar and Pompey. Pompey lost and had to flee to Egypt, where he was assassinated. Caesar's assassination followed closely on the fate of Pompey.

Now followed the civil wars in Rome, caused by Julius Caesar's political ambitions. The power struggle continued until 31 BC, when Caesar's adopted heir, Octavian, defeated Mark Antony at the Battle of Actium. Antony's defeat marked the end of the civil war and the end of the Roman Republic, but the start of the Roman Empire. Actium was the main battle of the Roman Civil War, fought on 2 September 31 BC. Octavian's fleet was commanded by Agrippa and Antony was supported by Cleopatra of Egypt. Octavian's defeat of Mark Antony earned him the title of Augustus from the senate.

The astronomer Ptolemy – also a geographer and mathematician – lived in Alexandria in Egypt, somewhere between AD 90 and 168. One of his greatest works was a study of the geography of the Roman world. Many of his maps were based on sound principles, but were limited by lack of accurate data and wrong assumptions about the size of the earth.

We turn now to Augustus's campaigns in Germania between 12 BC and AD 9. In 12 BC the Emperor Augustus had Gaul firmly under control and turned his sights on

Germany. He sent his adopted son Drusus to conquer and pacify the Germans – a campaign that was a success – and Publius Quintillius Varus became consul. He was described as being barely an administrator, and the result was the rebellion of AD 9. Varus mistakenly thought that Arminius, the rebel leader, was an ally, but Varus was ambushed together with three legions and three squadrons of auxiliary cavalry in the Teutoburg Forest, and the Roman soldiers were wiped out.

In AD 14 the Roman Empire was still in the process of expanding. Much territory had been added and consolidated by the time of Julius Caesar, but after his assassination in 44 BC, and the rise to power of Augustus, further territory was added. Although the senate was officially the government of the Roman Empire, Augustus was in fact the dictator of the empire for forty-one years. He had ended the civil wars and initiated a period of peace that lasted for more than 200 years. He carried out many reforms and was known as the father of his country. He died in AD 14.

By the first century AD the city of Rome had grown from a small agricultural community into a vast city. The government had had to adapt to this growth, and it was Augustus that was the driving force behind the project. He employed a police force and a fire brigade and built several aqueducts. He had the River Tiber dredged to prevent flooding. He spent massive sums looking after the city and making it the capital of a great empire. His claim was that when he arrived at Rome it was made of brick, and when he left it was made of marble.

What was the Roman Empire like in AD 68, the year of the death of the Emperor Nero? During his fourteen-year reign Nero focused much of his attention on diplomacy, trade and making Rome a great cultural capital. He also fought a successful war against the Parthian Empire and he improved ties with Greece. There was a military coup in AD 68, and Nero is said to have committed suicide. A civil war ensued, and the age was known as that of the four emperors, until Vespasian assumed power in AD 69. He was first emperor of the Flavian dynasty.

Let us take a look at the Roman North African city known as Leptis Magna. It is situated on the Mediterranean coast in the present-day Tripolitania region, originally founded by the Phoenicians in the tenth century BC. It became prominent in the fourth century BC after Carthage became a major power in the Mediterranean region, and it remained part of Carthage's dominions until the end of the Third Punic War in 146 BC, when it became part of the Roman Republic. From about 200 BC it operated very much as an independent city, but when Tiberius became emperor it became part of the Roman province of Africa, and it soon became a trading post of Roman Africa.

Eventually the Romans conquered Britain and remained there from AD 43 to 410. Hadrian's Wall was built after a visit to North Britain in AD 122. The purpose of the wall was to keep the barbarians at bay – the Picts of the Scottish Highlands – and to improve economic stability in the Roman province to the south. For many years Hadrian's Wall marked the northern limit of the Roman Empire. After Hadrian's death in 138 the new emperor abandoned Hadrian's Wall and built an earthwork wall to the north of Hadrian's Wall, 100 miles north of the original frontier. The northern tribes remained unconquered. The Emperor Marcus Aurelius abandoned the Antonine Wall and reoccupied Hadrian's Wall; it remained occupied until the Roman withdrawal from Britain in AD 410.

The Limes Germanicus, or Germanic Frontier, was a line of forts that operated between AD 83 and 260. At its height the line stretched from the North Sea into the Netherlands and eventually reached the Danube. The strength of the wall varied from location to location, but the fortifications were not effective in holding the barbarians at bay and preventing them from overthrowing the Roman Empire and its Pax Romana.

London, or Londinium, was established by the Romans soon after the invasion of Britain in AD 43. Initially it was a small trading town. It was sacked by Queen Boudicca around AD 63, after which the city was rebuilt as a planned Roman town, more populous than Colchester, as a capital. During the second century the city had a population of 35,000 to 60,000, but after AD 150 the population went into decline during an outbreak of the plague, from which it never fully recovered in Roman times. The famous Roman wall around the city was built somewhere between AD 190 and 225.

Between AD 66 and 70 the Jewish population revolted against the power of Rome, which did not take to the Judaic religion. A large number of Jews headed for more-peaceful Roman towns in further parts of the empire. The Romans did not like the Jews for they denied that the Roman emperor was a god, but in actual fact the Jews were able to practise their religion. The Roman emperor, Nero, sent his general, Vespasian, to overthrow the revolt.

Another revolt occurred between AD 69 and 70. After Nero had committed suicide in 68, the Emperor Vespasian and his son Titus went to crush the revolt. Titus fought the Jews until he won. One of the last holdouts was the fortress of Masada – here the Zealots held out against the Romans, who built a great ramp up the fortress, broke down the walls and destroyed the city. Tradition has it that the Zealots committed mass suicide rather than allow themselves to fall into Roman hands, but this is perhaps not true.

Another Jewish revolt occurred in AD 132: after three years of struggle the Jews were again defeated, at the fortress of Betar, in 135.

The years from about 1300 BC to AD 300 were the years of the Jewish diaspora. The word 'diaspora' refers to the scattering of the Jews around the world, often under duress. In 722 BC many were deported after the northern kingdom of Israel was conquered. By the time of the Roman invasion of Israel there were a number of Jewish communities scattered around the world. There were about one million Jews in Egypt and more than 7,000 in Rome. Following the great Jewish revolt of AD 66 to 70 and a later revolt, there were many deportations throughout the Roman world.

The years AD 45 to 300 saw the spread of the Catholic Church throughout the imperial lands. The great Roman roads facilitated the rapid spread of Christianity through the empire – the story is well told in the New Testament. By AD 40 a Christian community was established at Rome. The Great Fire of Rome was caused by the Christians – or so the Romans said. In spite of this Christianity continued to spread throughout the empire.

For the next 250 years the Catholic Church was either persecuted or became a persecutor, but eventually the Church was legitimized when the Emperor Constantine made it the state religion in 312. State-sponsored churches were built – for example St Peter's, Rome – and many were founded over the holy places of other religions.

The Dacian Wars, between 101 and 117, were short conflicts during the reign of the Emperor Trajan. The Dacians had always presented a threat to the Roman Empire, and Trajan prepared for war. The war only lasted for a few months, resulting in a great Roman victory, but before long the Dacians were again raiding Roman territory across the Danube, and this provoked a second war in 106. The Romans attacked the Dacian capital and burned it to the ground. These two great victories furthered Rome's expansionist policies and Trajan became known as a true and honourable civil emperor.

The Parthian Wars, 114 to 117, began as an attempt by the Parthian king, Ostroes, to impose his nephew as the next King of Armenia. The Roman Empire had imposed hegemony over Armenia for many years and had final authority in naming a king, so Trajan now headed east to Armenia in 114. Ostroes' nephew was deposed and the country was annexed as a Roman province. Trajan then moved south into Parthia, capturing Babylon and Ctesiphon until he reached the Persian Gulf. On his way back to Rome, Trajan fell ill following a defeat at the desert fortress of Hatra. He died in Selinus in 117.

By the second and third centuries the Roman Empire was under constant pressure from the Persians. At the Battle of Edessa the Emperor Valerian was captured and brutally put to death. Romans asked the King of Palmyra for assistance in their fight against the Persians, but he was assassinated and his wife took control. She won spectacular victories and eventually proclaimed herself Queen of Egypt. This was too much for the Romans, who captured her; she lived out the rest of her days in Rome.

The Sassanian Empire was another enemy of Rome – an empire that lasted from 224 to 651. The Sassanians were the last dynasty to rule Persia before the Arab conquest. The state religion was Zoroastrianism, and no other religions were tolerated. Christians were persecuted – when the Roman Empire became Christian, persecutions increased. The war with Rome started in 231, after the Sassanians had invaded Syria and looted Antioch. In a second war, in 260, the Roman emperor, Valerian, was captured and subjected to torture. Under later emperors Romans restored their fortunes, and in 298 the Sassanians gave up their struggle, and their territories in northern Mesopotamia were also annexed by Rome.

Roman control of Egypt started around 330. After the death of Cleopatra Egypt became a Roman-controlled province, but the Romans at this time did not interfere in the internal affairs of their conquered regions. In 314 Constantine made Christianity's Catholic Church the official religion of the Roman Empire and established a new capital at Constantinople. The Roman Empire was now divided and Egypt became part of East Rome. Egypt continued to be a centre of agriculture and commerce, but under the influence of Constantinople it gradually became more Greek and Asian. The Romans, of course, conquered Britain, controlling the island from AD 43 to 410. The Romans brought many innovations with them in the fields of construction, agriculture and industry, leaving a legacy that can be seen today. One example of this is the Roman roads – for example, Watling Street – which enabled the speedy movement of troops in the new province. Many modern highways follow the same routes as those impressive roads of ancient times – roads that were built nearly 2,000 years ago.

By 214 the Roman Empire was at the zenith of its power. It controlled vast territories and states, particularly around the Mediterranean. This was the period of the Severan dynasty, which lasted for about forty years, founded by Lucius Septimius Severus, and in a period when the court was influenced by formidable women. The last of the Severan dynasty was assassinated, which led to a period of civil war. The Pax Romana, which had been established by Augustus some 200 years earlier, finally began to crumble. The city of Rome's borders were being seriously challenged in the period from 235 to 312 – there were numerous assaults in the eastern provinces, and the Goths broke through the western frontiers on a number of occasions. In 260 they invaded Gaul and raiding parties reached as far as Spain.

Major invasions took place in Italy between 259 and 271. On all fronts the authority of the Roman Empire was being challenged. Between 270 and 273 new city walls were built to defend Rome against barbarian attacks. The period from 252 to 271 was a time of invasions and rebellions. In this century the Roman Empire went through a period of crisis. Valerian had been captured by the Persians, and his son was left in shaky control. At the same time the Goths were invading the northern borders in the east and Germanic tribes were attacking the borders to the west. Gaul, Britain and Espania felt neglected, so they decided to form a breakaway province. This Gallic Empire was quite successful, but after thirteen years it was pulled back into the empire proper. Let us take a look at the western breakaways, occupying the period from 262 to about 300. By the time of the Emperor Gallienus, Rome was failing to retain central control over the territory it had once held. In 260 the governor of Lower Germany led a rebellion and formed the Gallic Empire, which lasted for about fifteen years. This region was prosperous and self-sufficient, but it was eventually reabsorbed into the Roman Empire by Aurelian after a decisive battle.

We travel now to Palmyra, in the east, during the period from 260 to 273. Palmyra is a very ancient city founded by King Solomon; the Romans formally annexed it in 217 and gave it its name, which means city of the palms. In 260 the Persians overran several eastern Roman provinces, and the Emperor asked the King of Palmyra for help. The King was very successful, but in 267 he was assassinated; now his wife, Zenobia, took control and won many victories – she annexed a number of Roman territories and successfully invaded Egypt. This was too much for Aurelian, and Zenobia's army was defeated in 273. The overthrown queen was led in chains back to Rome.

Under the Emperor Diocletian the empire was reorganized between the years 284 and 295. In 292 he devised a system of tetrarchy, or rule by four caesars, where a senior emperor would rule in the west and another would rule in the east, and each would have a junior emperor under him, to be known as a caesar. He chose the eastern half of the empire for himself, and gave the western half to Maximian; this emperor divided his territory, making Constantius his junior. Diocletian retired in 305 and persuaded Maximian to do the same, but Maximian resumed his former political position in 307 following a coup promoted by Maximian's son, who had been overlooked in the succession. Still powerful, Diocletian again persuaded Maximian to stand down. Maximian again tried to assume power before being captured by Constantius's son, Constantine, but he died soon after.

Between the years 306 and 324 Constantine's elevation to ruler of the Roman Empire began when his father, Constantius, was nominated as junior emperor under Maximian, whom he succeeded as Augustus of the Western Empire in 305. When Constantius died in 306 his soldiers proclaimed Constantine as emperor, but he had a rival. The two met at the Battle of the Milvian Bridge, which Constantine won. Now Constantine became ruler of the Western Empire. In 324 he reunited the empire and spread Christianity throughout his realms. Constantine's capital was originally founded in the early days of the Greek colonial expansion, when it was called Byzantium. In the fourth century, having restored the unity of the empire, the Emperor was looking for a suitable capital in the east and chose Byzantium. He laid out and expanded the city, with a new central square called the Augusteum. The city was renamed Constantinople. Slowly the importance of Constantinople grew, but security was always an issue, and, following the death of the Emperor Valens and the defeat of the Roman armies by the Goths, a large defensive wall was built by the Emperor Theodosius in 413.

By 395 the Emperor Diocletian had divided the empire

into a western and eastern half, and each division was divided further; the result was four prefectures, which in turn were administered by four dioceses. By 395 it became difficult to defend the extremities of the empire – Britain's subjugation by Rome was running out of steam. Some legions had already been pulled back to defend the capital, and by the mid-fifth century provinces like Britain were left to their own devices.

The fifth century saw the rise of the Germanic kingdoms – all barbarians. There were enemies at the gates of Rome. The barbarians were now able to conquer former imperial lands, and the Huns and Goths launched many attacks on the frontiers of the crumbling and decadent empire. In Britain the Saxons saw their chance of keeping out the Romans if there was a change of political situation. Some countries remained as normal states within the Roman Empire, but many chased the legions out of their lands and set up independent kingdoms.

In the period from 527 to 565 the Emperor Justinian had a dream to unite the Roman Empire once again at Rome – the capital of the empire was now of course at Constantinople. But it was an impossible task, though his armies succeeded in reconquering lands in the western Mediterranean basin. As a Catholic Roman emperor he regarded it as his sacred duty to unite the former empire and consolidate the former gains of the Catholic Church. He is well remembered for his law reforms. Much more may have been achieved, but there was a crippling plague in 542. Justinian himself caught it, but made a recovery.

By 1453 the Roman Empire, or Byzantine Empire, was well in decline and was taken over by Islam. The history of this bureaucratic state is not very interesting, but the

Emperor was regarded as an absolute monarch who acted the role of God. The fall of Constantinople came in May 1453, bringing to an end East Rome. Moslems converted the Church of Santa Sophia to a mosque, which it remains to this day.

The Eternal City

Before we look at the history of spiritual Rome after political Rome's fall, it is useful to examine the history of the Greek world that preceded the Roman Empire – Rome borrowed many of its ideas from Athens. The head of the Greek Orthodox Church was the patriarch of Constantinople – a situation that exists to this day. Like the Roman Empire, the Catholic Church was a divided organisation, one part having Rome as its centre, the other centred at Constantinople in the Bosphoros.

Today political Rome has survived as Vatican City, whose head is the Pope. It has a population of about 1,000 and an area of 108 acres. The Vatican carries out a major role in international politics and has the spiritual care of over a billion people around the world. The Vatican has all the trappings of an independent state: it has its own army, currency, postal system and stamps, flag and anthem. The head of state is the Pope, who has a large private garden. There is a Vatican radio station and newspaper. Entrance to the state is limited by invitation only – usually for those on business directly linked to Vatican affairs. It also has overseas ambassadors, just like any other state.

The Vatican museums occupy a large area of Vatican City. They house the largest collection of classical and Renaissance art.

The Sistine Chapel is perhaps the greatest Vatican attraction. It is the official private chapel of the Pope, and is dedicated to the Virgin Mary. The wall paintings are by some of the greatest artists of the time. It was Michelangelo who painted the magnificent ceiling, commissioned by Pope Julius II. It took over four years to complete the ceiling, between 1508 and 1512. At an inaugural mass in 1512 everyone was amazed by this great work of classical art.

Just at the entrance to Vatican City the Vatican guard protects the Pope and other members of the Catholic Church from acts of violence. The Pontifical Swiss Guard is made up of Swiss Catholics, and its history may be traced back to the Middle Ages.

Both the Roman Empire and the Catholic Church look back to the city states of ancient Greece, and their imperial ambitions. Greek history, pagan in origin, dates back to the period from 750 to 400 BC – the age of early Attica. The Persians had occupied the peninsula upon which the state was situated, and the Athenians went about rebuilding the ancient walls that had been destroyed. This invited opposition from the Spartans and their allies, but the Athenians ignored the protests and carried on building. Despite fighting between Athens and Sparta, various Peloponnesian allies in the 460s continued work on the walls. New long walls connected Athens with the ports so that the city state would always have a supply of food and drink, and other supplies.

By the year 750 the world was well settled. Agrarian

economies had grown up along riverbanks – the Egyptian Empire being a famous example. This development led to the growth of trade and manufacturing industries. Other trappings of civilization followed, such as a hierarchical government, a legal system and the development of writing as a means of record-keeping.

Let us travel back to 2000 to 1250 BC to the Palace of Knossos in Minoan Crete. Excavations around Knossos show that the area had been inhabited since Neolithic times – perhaps before 6000 BC – and stood for 300 years until it was destroyed. It was rebuilt a number of times following a series of earthquakes. Each time the palace was rebuilt it became larger, until Knossos was a major city with an estimated 100,000 inhabitants. The king used the residence as a royal abode until at least 1380 BC. Minoan Crete lay many miles away in the eastern Mediterranean. Here villas for the wealthy started to appear in the rural landscape. They were perhaps the homes of wealthy landlords and were modelled after large palaces, with storage facilities, workshops and places of worship. Small towns started to develop near the palaces. There is also evidence of economic unity throughout the island. Women played an important role in Minoan society, and the gold artefacts, seals and spears that have been found point to a very rich upper class.

Mycenaean culture eventually declined and collapsed. For 500 years, from about 1600 BC, Mycenae was one of the major centres of Greek civilization. It was a military stronghold that dominated southern Greece, but by 1100 BC its powers eventually ended. Within a short time the palaces of southern Greece were burned – including that of Mycenae, which was abandoned by the twelfth century. There are a number of reasons why this was so, but none of them seem likely. It could have been due to sea raiders or even famine, but it may also have been due to large-scale invasions of the Dorian Greeks armed with iron weapons that overcame their bronze-equipped Mycenaean opponents. Another theory is that rivalry between individual city states ignited into all-out war. The period from 500 to 369 BC was the age of classical Greece and the Delian League – an association between the city states of Ionian Greece in the fifth century BC. Athens set the level of payment that each of these states had to pay, and they all became subject to Athenian dictators. At its height the Ionian Athenian Empire was composed of 172 tribute-paying states and it controlled the Aegean Sea. Many states that it controlled – for example, Sparta – felt very threatened by the growth of the Athenian Empire, and this developed into a very volatile situation in the mid-fifth century BC.

Let us take a look at the fortified city of Messene, situated on the south-west Peloponnese, founded in 369 BC after the liberation of Messene from Spartan rule. The city was constructed by the Thebans on the slopes of Mount Ithome. Its great stone walls are a tribute to Greek military engineering and perhaps they effectively sealed Sparta's doom. Messene became an independent city state, hostile to its former master; it cut its supply of slaves, and conscripts to the Spartan army. Having lost its supply of slaves, Sparta could no longer maintain a military presence. It was still capable of winning the occasional border skirmish, but was no longer a major player in the area.

The Greeks did not have any organized system of

religion or belief, but they had twelve major gods. These gods had temples in all the major cities, and some gods were associated with one particular place – for example, Apollo at Delphi and Zeus at Olympia. Rituals varied from site to site and within individual households. Smaller cults also developed based on the deeds of local heroes, who ranged from Olympic athletes to warriors, political leaders and temple leaders. The years between 900 and 435 BC saw the collapse of the Athenian Empire.

The Persians invaded Greece in 492 BC. They were finally defeated two years later, but another attempt was made in 481 BC. As a result the Delian League was formed under the leadership of Athens. At this time Greece was made up of city states, small in number, and they paid tribute to Athens. Athens began to grow in power, which concerned Sparta and led to the first Peloponnesian War, in 431 BC. Another war broke out sometime later, and it ended in victory for Sparta, and the complete defeat of Athens, in 404. Athens never regained its pre-eminence in the region, and Sparta dominated Greece for many years. The war marked the end of the golden age of classical Greece.

From 900 to 435 BC the Phoenicians and Greeks colonized the Mediterranean. The Phoenicians came from the city of Tyre and were a major trading power in the Mediterranean in the first millennium BC. They had trading contacts as far away as Egypt and Greece, and established colonies as far away as Spain, even reaching Britain. Their most successful colony was that of Carthage. Many of the Greek city states had colonies in the Mediterranean. Miletus, in Asia Minor, had ninety colonies scattered along the shores of the Black Sea.

In most colonies the motivation was to foster trade and further the interests of the mother city.

The seventh to the sixth centuries BC saw the rise of the Greek tyrannies, which were city states ruled by a single tyrant. These tyrants were generally installed by military coups, some of them having popular support in a sort of democratic age. The Greeks often turned to 'kings' or aristocrats when asked who they would prefer to rule over them.

Between 480 and 404 BC there were invasions into Greece from the north, but the invaders had to pass through Thessaly to reach southern Laconia, and doing so involved crossing a series of plains separated by mountain ranges. Thus Greece's natural terrain provided choke points, and at these points Greek phalanxes could be successfully deployed. Thus large parts of Greece were denied to an invader. The Spartans' stand at Thermopylae in 480 BC against the Persian Xerxes exemplifies this tactic. Xerxes' invasion of 480 BC, after much preparation, was held back by the Spartan King Leonidas for three days. The Persians eventually took the pass, but the delay gave the Athenians time to prepare for the decisive naval battle at Salamis that destroyed the Persian navy. The Persians left their army in Greece to fight one last battle at Plataea, where it suffered a major defeat by the Greeks, so ending the threat of Persian expansion into Europe.

Now followed the Peloponnesian War, between 431 and 404 BC, which was a defining point in the history of Greece. It was fought between Sparta and Athens; the first phase of the war saw repeated incursions by the Spartans in Attica, while Athens used its great naval strength to attack towns along the Peloponnesian coast. In 415 BC the second phase of the war began when Athens launched an attack on Syracuse, in Sicily, which was populated by settlers from Corinth. The final phase of the war was the defeat of Athens, as the result of an alliance between Sparta and Persia.

Between 382 and 336 BC Theban and Spartan campaigns took place. After the defeat of Athens by Sparta in 404 BC, the Spartans proved that its skills in civilian administration did not match up to its skills on the battlefield. Anyone that opposed them was executed, imprisoned or exiled. Sparta was hated. For some thirty years it had been a leading state in Greece, but it was now facing a different sort of world – Thebes was growing in influence and turned back a number of Spartan invasions. Eventually the two forces met at Leuctra, in 371. The result was indecisive, but Thebes was able to carve out an independent state for itself within Spartan territory. For a short time Macedonia became the most powerful state in the near east under the leadership of Alexander the Great, who conquered most of the known world, but it had started to expand after Philip II came to power in 359 BC. By 348 Philip had conquered Thrace and Chalcidice. Two years later Philip intervened in a war between Thebes and Phocis. A league now granted Macedonia the right to participate in Greek political issues and Philip was made commander in chief of all the league forces.

Athens became alarmed at the rise of Macedonia's power, but an alliance between Athens and Thebes was destroyed by Philip's army at Chaeronea in 338 BC, leaving Philip the master of Greece. While preparing an invasion of Persia, Philip was murdered, and he was succeeded by his son Alexander, who executed all those involved in his father's murder and any rivals or members of factions that might affect his position as king. Many people have heard of the empire of Alexander the Great – the nearest anyone else could come to a Roman emperor. His empire lasted from 336 to 323 BC and he is remembered as the conqueror of Persia along with many other regions in the near east; he even reached as far away as the Punjab. Alexander encouraged marriage between his own Greek people and the people that he subjected, uniting his army and the native populations.

Alexander died young, in 323 BC, possibly of malaria or West Nile virus, or from the consequences of heavy drinking. At the time of his death he was making plans to invade Europe. In about 273 BC Alexander's empire was divided. He had made no provision for his successor, and at the time of his sudden death his half-brother was mentally ill and his son was not yet born. The result was a power struggle, ending in the collapse of central power in Greece and beyond.

Finally let us return to the Roman Empire when the Roman and Greek world witnessed the crucifixion of Jesus Christ. Christians were persecuted by the Roman Empire, and eventually they became persecutors of all other faiths. The Stations of the Cross tell the story of how the Roman Empire sent Jesus to His death upon a cross, His hands and feet nailed to the wood.

The mission of Jesus Christ in the world is well told in the New Testament, but let us examine the first Station of the Cross: Jesus having been beaten and spat upon was now condemned to death. He had been whipped and mocked and called the King of the Jews.

The second Station of the Cross tells how Jesus had to take up His Cross, a large heavy piece of wood, on His way to Calvary to be killed as a common criminal. He is said to have been in His late twenties or early thirties when He met His death. Pontius Pilate, the Roman governor of Judaea, said that he could find no fault with Jesus, but he nevertheless handed Him over to the Jews, who demanded His death.

The third Station of the Cross tells how Jesus fell for the first time beneath the Cross. The crowds mocked him, but His mission to the Roman Empire was strong to bring the word to all peoples, and to eventually bring about the conversion of the Emperor to the Catholic Church. His disciples watched His agony as He took up the Cross again. Peter, whom Jesus had made leader of the Church, watched as his Lord made His way to the hill of Calvary. Christ met His mother, who all the time observed her Son's passion; for an instant they saw each other, but Jesus shouldered the Cross and proceeded to His death. Mary, the virgin, had been conceived without the taint of original sin (immaculate conception) to bear Jesus, for God had intervened in the course of history to make Mary the mother of the God-Man talked about in the Old Testament. Jesus' beliefs struck at the basis of the Roman Empire and its emperors, who were said to be divine.

The fifth Station of the Cross tells how Jesus fell again, and was helped by Simon of Cyrene. At this point Jesus' physical strength failed Him, and He could go no further. The Romans insisted that Simon should carry the Cross to Calvary, and still Jesus was put upon and mocked. Mary must have felt quite helpless as she saw her Son fall.

The sixth Station of the Cross tells a story of spiritual love: Jesus met Veronica as He proceeded up the hill to Calvary, His face covered in sweat. Veronica wiped Jesus' face, and on the cloth the imprint was made of the Messiah's countenance.

He had for a while taken up His Cross, but again He fell – the seventh Station of the Cross. He was losing much blood at every step. He fell to the ground, unable to go on. All the time He prayed to God, and was sure that God would raise Him from the dead after the long period of suffering on the Cross.

The Messiah at the eighth Station of the Cross comforted the women of Jerusalem. They cried out at the sight of Jesus' suffering on His journey to death. But Jesus turned to them and said that they were daughters of Jerusalem, and that they should not weep on His account. They should weep for themselves and for their children. He told the women not to weep for Him, for He was the Lamb of God, and was dying for the sins of all the world.

The ninth Station of the Cross tells how Jesus fell again almost at His destination with death, just before the spot of His Crucifixion. He was whipped on by the cruel Roman soldiery.

At last Jesus reached Calvary, by which time midday approached. He was stripped and drenched with gall; He would soon make His sacrifice. The Romans began to prepare Him for the Cross. His garments had been blood-soaked by the whipping, and only a small cloth covered His private regions. This is the tenth Station of the Cross.

The eleventh Station of the Cross tells how Jesus was nailed to the Cross, which had been laid on the ground, and Jesus stretched upon it. His hands and feet were nailed to the wood. His mother, Mary, sat at the foot of the Cross and Jesus cried out, "Woman, behold your Son." Jesus must have known that death would soon come, but in His terrible state this seemed an eternity away.

Now Jesus died upon His Cross (the twelfth Station of the Cross) after waiting three hours for death. During this time He prayed for His murderers and promised paradise to a penitent robber that stood next to Him and another criminal. All was now finished, and the Messiah bowed His head and gave up the ghost.

The thirteenth Station of the Cross tells how Jesus was taken down from the Cross and laid against Mary's bosom. The watchers of the Crucifixion had made their way home after there was a total eclipse of the sun. Then Joseph of Arimathea and Nicodemus took Jesus' body away for burial, and placed it in the arms of His mother.

At last we come to the fourteenth Station of the Cross, which tells how Jesus was laid in a tomb. He only remained there for three days. The tomb was closed, but again God intervened in the course of history, for Jesus was resurrected from the dead. The tomb was open and only His burial clothes were visible.

Jesus appeared before Mary Magdalene, who had kept watch over the tomb. He also appeared to His mother and assured her that she would be raised into heaven as the mother of God. Christ then appeared before His disciples on the shores of the Sea of Galilee, where they were catching fish, and exhorted them to go forth and teach all nations in the name of the Father, Son and Holy Spirit.

As Rome was the capital of the Roman Empire, the world's first superpower, St Peter established the Catholic Church there and became its first leader, or Pope. Around the year 80, Peter was buried on Vatican Hill, and this humble spot soon became a place of pilgrimage for all Christians throughout the widespread Roman Empire.

The first St Peter's Basilica was opened in 326 and witnessed a number of visits from Europe's post-Roman kings. It survived the many sackings of Rome in the early medieval period. In 1376 attempts were made to restore Rome to its former glory as the centre of the Catholic Church. The planning for a replacement church started under Pope Nicholas, in 1452, but it was not until 1506 that the first stone was laid by Pope Julius II, a soldier Pope. The basilica was built over a period of 100 years. Michelangelo painted the ceiling of the Sistine Chapel over sixteen years, finishing it at the age of seventy-two.

St Peter's is the largest church in the world, standing at 600 feet long and 450 feet wide at the transepts, covering a floor area of six acres and capable of housing 8,000 people. From ground level to the top of the cross on the dome is 360 feet. It contains forty-four altars, 395 statues, 778 columns and ninety-nine oil lamps that burn day and night round the tomb of the Apostle. The basilica was consecrated in 1626 by Pope Urban VIII. St Peter's Square is one of the wonders of the modern age, and comes to life at Christmas and Easter when the Pope delivers his blessing. In the centre of the square is the Egyptian obelisk brought back to Rome by the Emperor Caligula to grace the Circus of Nero; it reaches 150 feet into the sky, and its top is said to contain a fragment of the True Cross. St Peter's Basilica, along with the Imperial Circus Maximus and the Colosseum, (the great amphitheatre) is visible to all visitors to the Eternal City – a city that has lived for hundreds of years. Today the modern mind has a sneaking admiration for the Rome of its emperors and its many popes, who live on in the Roman traditions. Hail, Caesar! And hail to the popes of the Eternal City! Hail Mary, mother of God.

Select Bibliography

Charles Burns, *The Election of a Pope* (Catholic Truth Society, 1997).

David Baldwin, *Rome* (Catholic Truth Society, 2005).

Donald Attwater with Catherine Rachel John, *Saints* (Penguin, 1995).

Ian Barnes, *Classical World* (Eagle, 2007).

J. N. D. Kelly, *The Oxford Dictionary of Popes* (Oxford, 1986).

John Henry Newman, *Meditations on the Stations of the Cross* (Catholic Truth Society, 1991).

Maxwell Staniforth, *Early Christian Writings* (Penguin, 1968).

Mel Gibson, *The Passion* (Tan Books, 2004).

Michael Sheane, *The Twilight Pagans* (1990).